Words Have Power

Words Have Power

Dr. Ashutosh Karnatak

DIVE IN THE OCEAN OF KNOWLEDGE
Ocean Books
Ocean Books Pvt. Ltd.
ISO 9001:2015 Publishers

Published by
Ocean Books (P) Ltd.
4/19 Asaf Ali Road,
New Delhi-110 002 (INDIA)
e-mail: info@oceanbooks.in

ISBN 978-81-8430-259-2
Words Have Power
by. Dr. Ashutosh Karnatak

Edition
2023

Price
₹ 200.00 (Rupees Two Hundred only)

Printed at
Narula Printers, Delhi

Preface

You are what you read, think, analyze and ultimately do. It's already been established through many studies and experiments that words affect your behavior. One such experiment was conducted to find out whether words have a psychological effect on people's moods or not by bringing three groups and giving each of them a word based puzzle to solve.

"The first group was given a puzzle that had words like "calm" and "polite", the second group was given a puzzle that had words like "anger" and "rude" while the third group was given a puzzle that had neutral words.

Right after solving the puzzle they were all asked to leave to another room and on their way they found someone who kept interrupting them and forcing them to wait for a long time. The first group of people who were exposed to the polite words was more polite to the person who wasted their time. The second group of people who were exposed to the rude words was found to respond more aggressively to the person who wasted their time while the third group had a neutral response."

From the experiment, it can be seen that words affect your thinking and thereby your behavior. This is due to the fact that words get momentarily imprinted on your mind. Consider the case of electric current that after its passage leaves some charge for sometime in the surrounding. Similarly, the words leave some temporary effect in the mind after you get exposed to them. If you are constantly doing the self-affirmations i.e. repeating the same words to yourself repeatedly, you could imagine the potential long-term effect on your behavior.

Numerous studies in Psychology particularly **'Positive Psychology'** have corroborated this fact. The thoughts that come to your conscious mind comprises of words, sentences and mental images. Words and thoughts that stay longer slip into the subconscious mind. It means what you start feeding your subconscious mind continuously as raw material gets processed by it and delivered as the final product in the form of your own behavior and actions. Therefore, what you repeatedly think and thereafter perform becomes your habit and ultimately your character.

As a corollary, a study published in the **Journal of Personality and Social Psychology** also suggests:

You may actually end up changing your own behavior and thoughts to match what you constantly read.

Words therefore have power to heal, the power to destroy, and the power to change the world. With this view in mind, a self-help book has been created consisting of 26 desirable attributes (akin to 26 English alphabets), to be inculcated and promoted in your own behavior to lead a happy life. At the end of the book is the compendium of some stories that are interesting as well as inspirational. This book, therefore, is an endeavor toward enlivening your spirit, for a hale and hearty generation must have a healthy body, consummate mind as well as cheery spirit.

– Dr. Ashutosh Karnatak

Contents

PART - I

Read ABCD Again

A T T I T U D E

1 + 20 + 20 + 9 + 20 + 21 + 4 + 5 =

100

Attitude

Meaning

The way a person views something or tends to behave towards, it is known as attitude. Your attitude determines your altitude. Positive attitude in life helps us decide whether or not a particular thing or person is going to affect our life positively.

Story

Thomas Alva Edison made some of the greatest inventions in the world, and the light bulb is one of them.

He tried 2000 different materials in search of a filament for the light bulb. But nothing seemed to support the electricity generated. None of these filaments worked satisfactory. His assistant complained, "All our work is in vain, there is no use of it. We haven't learned anything."

Edison smiled and replied confidently, "Oh, we have come a long way and we have learned so much. Now we know that there are 2000 elements that cannot be used to make a good light bulb."

Thomas Edison held a world record of 1093 patents for inventions. His attitude toward his failure made him achieve that feat.

"Attitude is a little thing that makes a big difference."

—Winston Churchill

Brand

Meaning

It means to give a product a distinctive identity by means of characteristic design, packaging, etc.

Similarly, we should look for opportunities to develop ourselves as a brand by developing good and distinctive qualities. Like a good brand is known and trusted for its superior qualities over others, one should try and set themselves apart too.

Story

One day, there was a blind man sitting on the steps of a building with a hat by his feet and a sign that read: "I am blind, please help".

A creative publicist was walking by and stopped to observe. He saw that the blind man had only a few coins in his hat. He dropped in more coins and, without asking for permission, took the sign and rewrote it.

He returned the sign to the blind man and left. That afternoon the publicist returned to the blind man and noticed that his hat was full of bills and coins.

The blind man recognized his footsteps and asked if it was he who had rewritten his sign and wanted to know what he had written on it.

The publicist responded, "Nothing that was not true. I just wrote the message a little differently." He smiled and went on his way.

The new sign read: 'Today is Spring and I cannot see it.'

Sometimes we need to change our strategy, i.e. how we brand ourselves. If we always do what we've always done, we'll always get what we've always gotten.

Sometimes It's not WHAT we say; It's HOW we say it!!

– Anonymous

❑

Concentration

Meaning

Directing of the attention or the mental faculties toward a single object.

Story

One day, some youths went to a *jungle* to practice shooting. They kept few pots at a distance and targeted them. None of them could hit even a single pot.

A saint who was watching them started laughing. One of them went to him and asked, "Why are you laughing? Do you know how to shoot?"

At this, the saint took the gun and fired at the pots and smashed all of them one by one. The youths were amazed to see this and asked the saint if he was a magician.

The saint replied, "I am neither a magician nor a sharpshooter. I just concentrated and the result is in front of you. One should always work with concentration."

The youths thanked him for the piece of advice.

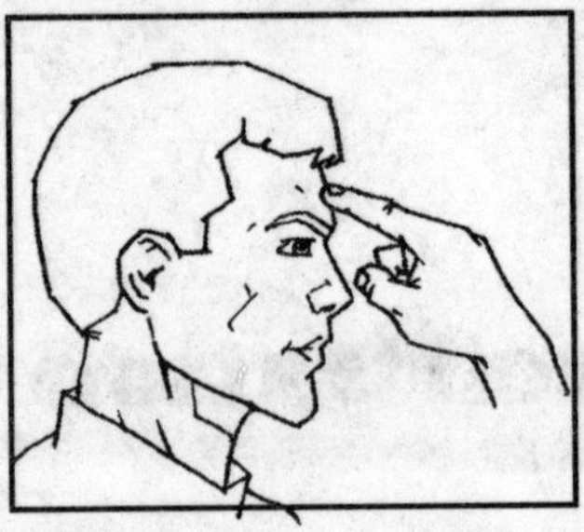

Before water generates steam, it must reach a temperature of 100°C; heat of even 99°C will not do it. The water must boil to generate enough steam to move an engine. Similarly, success in any endeavour requires single-minded attention to detail and total concentration.

❑

Desire

Meaning

To express a wish or make a request for.

It is important to have a desire. It helps you understand what you want, and when you know what you truly desire, you can set goals to achieve it. Desire gives a person the courage to say, "I'm good, but not as good as I should be."

Ordinary people say, "I'm not as bad as a lot of other people." A person with desire makes commitments; other people make promises.

Story

Once upon a time, there lived a giant named Happy, in the hills. He did not have any friends, as everybody thought that he was big and scary. So nobody tried being friends with him. When he saw kids playing in a nearby village, he too wanted to play with them. He had a desire of being friends with everybody so that he won't have to live alone.

One day it rained very heavily, and it almost flooded the village. The villagers ran to the place where Happy lived. Happy had a big house so invited them all in. When the rain got over, Happy helped the villagers rebuild their houses. And with Happy's help the village was turned into new. Happy's biggest desire was to have friends and he fulfilled his desire by being nice to everybody and helping them. Now nobody was scared of him and he was truly happy.

"If you greatly desire something, have the guts to stake everything on obtaining it."

— Brendan Francis

❑

Efficient

Meaning

Performing or functioning in the best possible manner with the least waste of time and effort.

It is important to know that whatever you do, do it the best way. Just like you squeeze out every bit of toothpaste to get the most out of the tube, you must push yourself to the limit to excel in your area of interest.

Story — The Three Little Pigs

Once upon a time, there were three little pigs and the time came for them to leave home and seek their fortunes.

Before they left, their mother told them "Whatever you do, do it the best that you can because that's the way to get along in the world. The first little pig built his house out of straw because it was the easiest thing to do. The second little pig built his house out of sticks. This was a little bit stronger than a straw house. The third little pig built his house out of bricks.

One night the big bad wolf, who dearly loved to eat fat little piggies, came along and saw the first little pig in his house of straw. He said "Let me in, let me in, little pig or I'll huff and I'll puff and I'll blow your house in!"

"Not by the hair of my chinny chin chin", said the little pig.

But of course the wolf did blow the house in and ate the first little pig.

The wolf then came to the house of sticks.

"Let me in, let me in little pig or I'll huff and I'll puff and I'll blow your house in". "Not by the hair of my chinny chin chin", said the little pig. But the wolf blew that house in too, and ate the second little pig.

The wolf then came to the house of bricks.

"Let me in , let me in" cried, the wolf.

"Or I'll huff and I'll puff till I blow your house in".

"Not by the hair of my chinny chin chin", said the pig.

Well, the wolf huffed and puffed but he could not blow down that brick house. But the wolf was a sly old wolf and he climbed up on the roof to look for a way into the brick house.

The little pig saw the wolf climb up on the roof and lit a roaring fire in the fireplace and placed on it a large kettle of water.

When the wolf finally found the hole in the chimney he crawled down and splashed right into that kettle of water and that was the end of piggy's troubles with the big bad wolf.

The next day the little pig invited his mother over. She said "You see it is just as I told you. The way to get along in the world is to do things as well as you can." Fortunately, for that little pig, he learned that lesson. And he just lived happily ever after!

Just do your best, let God Do the rest.

"By concentrating our efforts upon a few major goals, our efficiency soars, our projects are completed, and we are going somewhere."

—Michael Korda

Focus

Meaning

A central point, as of attraction, attention, or activity.

In life, it is important to have focus. Focus helps you concentrate on things more important than others. And when you know what you want, it becomes easier to achieve them.

Success = Focus × Intelligence × Time

Therefore, even with average intelligence, one can increase his likelihood of success by having superior focus and apportioning more time in the field he wants to excel in. The point is to find out where your passion lies. Other things will automatically fall in the right place.

Story

When Guru Dronacharya started to teach his students about Archery, he placed a bird on a tree and asked them aim at the bird's eye. When the first student stretched his bow to take his aim, Guru asked him, "What do you see?", the student said "I see the garden, the tree, the flowers, everything!" and then the student was asked to lower his bow and not to shoot. The next student stepped ahead and he asked him the same question, the student answered, "I see the air blowing the leaves of the tree".

Then came Arujna, when he was asked what he saw, he said, "The only thing I can see is the bird's eye". The Guru asked him to release his bow, and it hit the bird's eye.

"Good performance is about the capacity to focus and concentrate."

– Betty Buckley

❑

Goal

Meaning

The aim or object towards which an endeavour is directed.

Goals help us decide what we have to achieve. They also help us decide the end point of a journey.

Story

The first time Ram heard about the Island of Inventions, he was still very young. But the wonders he heard about sounded so incredible to him that they were forever engraved in his memory. Ever since he was a little boy, he never stopped searching for clues to investigate—Clues which might lead him to that wonderful place. He read hundreds of adventure books, histories, volumes of physics and chemistry; even music.

Taking a little from here, a little from there, he arrived at quite a clear idea of what the Island of Inventions was really like. It was a secret place, where all the great wise men of the world would meet to learn and invent together. Access to the island was totally restricted. To be able to join that select club, you ought to have created some great invention for humanity. Only then could you receive the unique and special invitation—which came with instructions on how to get to the island.

To be in with a chance, Ram spent the years of his youth studying and inventing. Every new idea he got, he made it into an invention, and if there were ever anything he didn't understand, he would seek out someone who could help him. Soon he met other young people, brilliant inventors too, and he told them of the secrets and marvels of the Island of Inventions. These fellow young inventors would likewise dream of being sent the letter, which is how the invitation was referred to.

As time passed, the disappointment of not being sent the letter gave rise to even greater collaboration and mutual help between the young inventors. Their interesting individual inventions were put together, creating some incredible contraptions. They met in Ram's house, which ended up looking like a huge warehouse for machines and spare parts. Their inventions became known throughout the world, and managed to improve every aspect of life.

But even after all that, no invitation came.

They did not lose heart. They continued learning and inventing every day, trying to come up with more and better ideas. Fresh young talent was added to their group, as more and more inventors dreamed of getting to the island. One day, a long time later, Luca, already very old, was speaking with a brilliant young man who had written to him to try to join the group. Luca told the young man the great secret of the Island of Inventions, and of how he was sure that some day they would receive an invitation. Surprised, the young inventor interrupted Ram:

"What? You mean this isn't really the Island of Inventions? Isn't the letter you sent me the real invitation?"

And, as old as he was, Luca looked around him, and realized that his dream had become true in his very own house. He realized that no island could exist which would be better than where he was now. No place of invention would be better than what he and his friends had created. Ram felt happy to know that he had always been on the island, and that his life of invention and study had been a truly happy one.

"People with goals succeed because they know where they're going."

—Earl Nightingale

❑

Hope

Meaning

The feeling that what is wanted can be had or that events will turn out for the best.

It is important to have hope. It gives the courage to keep moving on the same path. Hope helps us work hard with a belief that whatever we desire we will get with hard work.

Story

Rita was a daughter of an army man. Her father was a soldier in the army. And she loved her father a lot. Her father was most of the time awayon border protecting the nation from the enemy.

So whenever he would come back, they would sit for hours together and talk. He would bring her a lot of toys and chocolates, and would tell her the tales of the border. For Rita, her Dad was a Hero who protects everybody from the people who want to harm them.

One day while her father was back home for his yearly vacation, she was playing with him. And suddenly her father received a call from the army and he was asked to come back, as the neighbouring country had attacked us.

Her father left and when the war was over Rita's mother was told that her father had been missing and can't be found anywhere.

But her father had promised that after the war was over he would come back home to her. So when her mother was crying, she asked her not to lose hope as her father had promised her that he would come back.

Rita wrote a letter to the army to not stop looking for him as she had a hope that he will be found somewhere in the mountains, because the last time he wrote a letter to her he spoke about the mountains.

The army went looking for her father in the mountains, and there in a small hut an old lady and her family were taking care of her father. They said he had been unconscious for six months.

Her father was brought back home, and everybody said that Rita's hope kept her father alive.

HOPE

is the little voice you hear whisper "maybe" when it seems the entire world is shouting No!"

"Many of the great achievements of the world were accomplished by tired and discouraged men who kept on working."

– Anonymous

❑

Intelligence

Meaning

Capacity for learning, reasoning, understanding, and similar forms of mental activity; aptitude in grasping truths, relationships, facts, meanings, etc.

Story

Once upon a time, there were two incredibly intelligent and capable boys. Their wonderful talents were obvious from an early age, and they easily outdid everyone around. They had always known they were special, and they harboured inside them a desire that, in the future, everyone would come to admit how exceptional they were.

Each of them developed in a different way. The first used all his talent and intelligence to have a successful career and show everyone his superiority. He took part in all kinds of competitions, visited all the most important people and places, and was great at making friends in high places. Even when still very young, no one doubted that some day he would be the wisest and most important person in the land.

The second boy, equally aware of his own capabilities, never stopped feeling a heavy responsibility. He would do almost any task better than those around him, and he would feel obliged to help them. This didn't leave him enough time to follow his own dreams of greatness. He was always busy looking for ways to more effectively help others. As a result, he was a much-loved and well-known person, but only in his own small circle.

Destiny was such that a great disaster struck that land, spreading problems and misery far and wide. The first of those brilliant young men had never come across anything like this, but his brilliant ideas worked successfully throughout the land, and they managed to slightly improve the situation. But the second young man was so used to solving all kinds of problems, and had such useful know-how in certain subjects, that the disaster hardly affected the people in his region at all. His admirable methods were then adopted across the land, and the fame of this good and wise man spread even more than had that of the first young man. Indeed, he was soon elected Governor of the whole nation.

The first young man then understood that the greatest fame and wisdom is that which is born from the very things we do in life, from the impact they have on others, and from the need to improve ourselves every day. He never again took part in competitions or vain shows, and from thereon, whenever he travelled, he took his books along with him, so he would be ready always to offer a helping hand to all.

"It is not enough to have a good mind; the main thing is to use it well."

—Rene Descartes

❑

Justice

Meaning

The quality of being just; righteousness, equitableness, or moral rightness.

It is important to be just and right. And to be just, one should be fair to people around him.

Story – Aditi's Justice to the Bully

Aditi had joined a new school. She and her new friends had lunch in the school playground every day. One day, the school bully came to them.

"What are you having for lunch?", he asked the children rudely. The children were afraid of the bully. They silently passed their lunch boxes to him. The bully looked into the lunch boxes one by one. He saw that Aditi had brought vegetable noodles.

"Give it to me," he said, grabbing the lunch box from Aditi's hands.

She was shocked. "How long has he been doing this?", she asked.

"For some time now," said the other children after the bully had left. "He hits us if we refuse!"

Aditi was angry. "I won't let him bother us again," she said. "Wait till you see what I do tomorrow!"

She went home and told her mother to give her two boxes of lunch the next day. Aditi told her what she wanted for lunch.

The next day, the bully came and took Aditi's lunch box. It was the box with the special lunch, just for him!

In a few seconds, the children heard the bully cry out in pain.

And then he threw the lunch box away.

"I asked my mother to make food full of chilly, and now I am sure that bully will not bother any kid ever."

"If we expect others to rely on our fairness and justice we must show that we rely on their fairness and justice."

–Calvin Coolidge

❑

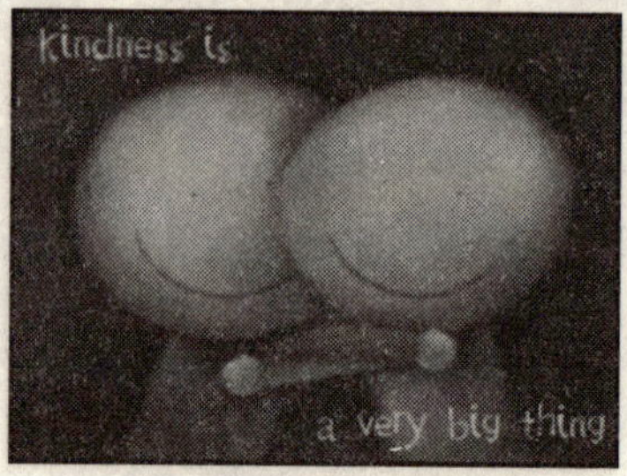

Kindness

Meaning

A kind, considerate, or helpful act.

It is important to be kind, because an act of kindness is never forgotten. And every act of kindness is rewarded in a similar way.

Story

A little boy about 10 years old was standing before a shoe store on roadway, barefoot, peering through the window, and shivering with cold. A lady approached the boy and said, "My little fellow, why are you looking so earnestly in that window?"

"I was asking God to give me a pair of shoes," was the boy's reply.

The lady took him by the hand and went into the store, and asked the clerk to get half a dozen pairs of socks for the boy. She then asked if he could give her a basin of water and a towel, which he quickly brought to her. She took the little fellow to the back part of the store and, removing her gloves, knelt down, washed his little feet and dried them with a towel.

By this time the clerk had returned with the socks. Placing a pair upon the boy's feet, she also purchased him a pair of shoes. After tying up the remaining pairs of socks, she gave them to him. She patted him on the head and said, "No doubt, my little fellow, you feel more comfortable now?" As she turned to go, the astonished lad caught her by the hand, and looking up in her face, with tears in his eyes, answered the question with these words: "Are you God's wife?"

"A little thought and a little kindness are often worth more than a great deal of money."

—John Ruskin

❑

Love

Meaning

A tender feeling toward another.

The more we care for the happiness of others, the greater our own sense of well-being becomes. Cultivating a close, warm-hearted feeling for others puts the mind at ease. This gives us the strength to cope with any obstacles we encounter.

Story

Long ago in India, there lived a young boy by the name of Mohan.

One winter's night, Mohan's mother developed a high fever. She could not sleep and was feeling very restless. In the middle of the night, she felt thirsty and asked her son to fetch a glass of water.

Mohan got up immediately and went to the kitchen to fetch the glass of water for his beloved mother.

To his dismay, he found the water pot empty. In those days, there was no running water in the homes. One could not just turn on the tap in the house to obtain drinking water; they had to carry water from the well or spring for drinking and other daily use.

Mohan was in a dilemma. Should he tell his mother that there was no water left in the pot and ask her to wait till morning when their cook would fetch water from the spring? It would mean that his mother would not be able to quench her thirst till the morning. Could Mohan bear seeing his mother suffer for so long? No, never!

So he left the house that cold night and went to the village spring to fetch water. He filled the pot with water and carried the heavy pot all the way back home. When he reached the house, he quickly poured the water into a glass and brought it to his mother. However, when he entered her room, he found his mother fast asleep.

Mohan was again in a dilemma. Should he wake his mother up to drink or should he just let her sleep through? Well, Mohan decided not to wake her up. He sat in a chair by her bedside holding the glass of water with both hands to make sure he did not spill it.

When his mother woke up a while later, she found, to her great surprise, Mohan sitting by her bedside holding a glass of water in his hands. When Mohan saw that his mother was awake, he quickly handed the glass of water to her with much care. He said: "Sorry I was not able to give you the water earlier. I went to the well to get the water and was waiting for you to wake up so I could give it to you."

Mohan's mother drank the glass of water with gratitude and pride. She truly knew then how much her son loved her and was deeply moved by his compassionate act.

"A flower cannot blossom without sunshine, and man cannot live without love."

—Max Muller

❑

The best make-up is Smile.

The best jewelry is Modesty.

The best clothing is Confidence.

Modesty

Meaning

Marked by simplicity; humble in spirit or manner; free from ostentation or pretension.

An attitude of modesty is important to learning, to intellectual growth and development. Arrogance and pride stand in the way of learning from others.

Story

Once upon a time, a very long time ago, the four-footed animals made the lion their king. There was a gigantic fish that roamed the oceans, and the fish made him their king. The birds were attracted to beauty, so they chose the Golden Swan as their king.

King Golden Swan had a beautiful golden daughter. While she was still young, he granted her one wish. She wished that, when she was old enough, she could pick her own husband.

When his daughter was old enough, King Golden Swan called all the birds living in the vast Himalayan Mountains of Central Asia to a gathering. The purpose was to find a worthy husband for his golden daughter. Birds came from far away, even from high Tibet. There were geese, swans, eagles, sparrows, humming birds, cuckoos, owls and many other kinds of birds.

The gathering was held on a high rock slab, in the beautiful green land of Nepal. King Golden Swan told his lovely daughter to select whichever husband she wished.

She looked over the many birds. Her eye was attracted by a shining emerald-green long-necked peacock, with gorgeous flowing tail feathers. She told her father, "This bird, the peacock, will be my husband."

Hearing that he was the lucky one, all the other birds crowded around the peacock to congratulate him. They said, "Even among so many beautiful birds, the golden swan princess has chosen you. We congratulate you on your good fortune."

The peacock became so puffed up with pride that he began to show off his colorful feathers in a fantastic strutting dance. He fanned out his spectacular tail feathers and danced in a circle to show off his beautiful tail. Being so conceited, he pointed his head at the sky and forgot all modesty, so that he also, showed his most private parts for all to see!

The other birds, especially the young ones, giggled. But King Golden Swan was not amused. He was embarrassed to see his daughter's choice behave in this way. He thought, "This peacock has no inner shame to give him proper modesty. Nor does he have the outer fear to prevent indecent behaviour. So why should my daughter be shamed by such a mindless mate?"

Standing in the midst of the great assembly of birds, the king said, "Sir peacock, your voice is sweet, your feathers are beautiful, your neck shines like an emerald, and your tail is like a splendid fan. But you have danced here like one who has no proper shame or fear. I will not permit my innocent daughter to marry such an ignorant fool!"

Then King Golden Swan married his golden daughter to a royal nephew. The silly strutting peacock flew away, having lost a beautiful wife.

> WORK FOR A CAUSE, NOT FOR APPLAUSE. LIVE LIFE TO EXPRESS, NOT TO IMPRESS. DON'T STRIVE TO MAKE YOUR PRESENCE NOTICED JUST MAKE YOUR ABSENCE FELT
> -Unknown

"If you let pride go to your head, you'll wind up acting like a fool."

—Anonymous

❑

> It is nice to be important, but it is more important to be nice.

Nice

Meaning

Being considerate and helpful when it is needed to each other.

Being nice when it is needed to each other is what brings peace and happiness to ours and each other's lives.

Story

Once upon a time there, was a good, cheerful wizard who loved to use his magic to make everyone happy. He was also quite an unusual wizard because he was allergic to a load of different foods. He had to be very careful what he put in his mouth. He was always being invited to parties, and he would always gladly accept, because he always had new tricks and games to try out.

In the beginning, everyone was considerate about his allergies, and they took special care to prepare food that he would be able to eat safely. But as time went on, people tired of having to prepare special foods for him. They began to forget his dietary requirements. After having enjoyed his magic, people would leave him by himself, and the parties became less enjoyable. Sometimes they didn't even bother to tell him what was in the food, and, more than once, he ended up with a black tongue, a red face, and a very itchy body.

Angry at such lack of consideration, he waved his wand and cast a huffy spell that gave everyone a special allergy. Some became allergic to birds or frogs, others to fruit or meat, some to raindrops.... And so, each person had to take special care from then on. Whenever people met up to eat or have a party, they ended up having to go to the doctor.

Ending parties in this way was such a pain that, gradually, people began making an effort to learn what each other's allergies were. Now they would prepare everything carefully, so that they could have a good time together without getting sick. Visits to the doctor decreased, and in less than a year, life in town returned to normal, filled with parties and celebrations, always attended by the wizard, who gave life and joy to the occasion. Even better, now he could stay and enjoy the whole party. No one would have suspected that, in that town, every single person was strongly allergic to something.

Some time later, without anyone knowing, the wizard waved his wand again and undid the spell. The people had learned well how to be considerate towards others, and how they could enjoy each others' company even better just by making a little effort to adapt to each and every person.

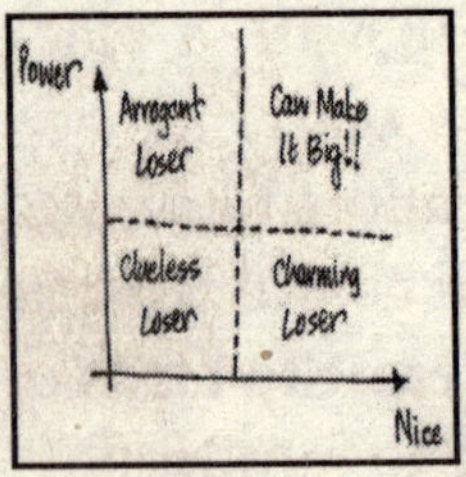

Being nice to someone you dislike doesn't mean you're a fake. It means you are mature enough to tolerate your dislike towards them.

– Anonymous

❑

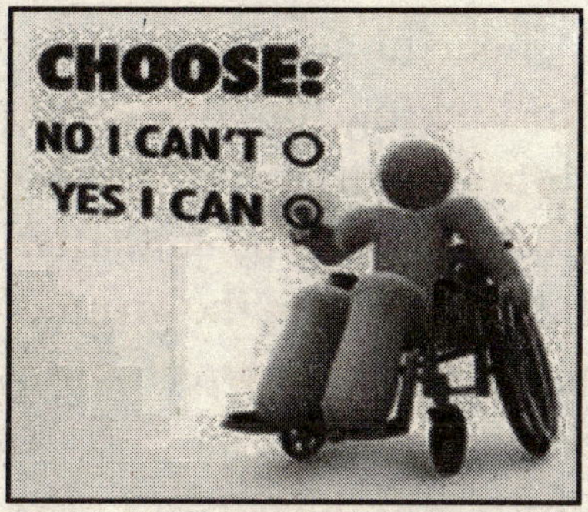

Optimism

Meaning

An inclination to put the most favourable construction upon actions and events or to anticipate the best possible outcome.

Optimism helps us accomplish our task with full enthusiasm, which in turn, helps us complete the job in hand with perfection.

Story

There was once a farmer who devised a competition between his dog and his rabbit. He made a hole in one of his biggest fields, and hid a carrot and a bone in it. He wanted to see which animal would find them first.

The rabbit was very cheerful and optimistic, and he threw himself into looking for the carrot, digging here and there, totally convinced that he would find it. But the dog was pessimistic, and after sniffing around for a bit, he lay down on the ground and began to complain how difficult it was to find one bone in such a big field.

The rabbit dug for hours, and with every new hole the dog complained even more about how difficult this was, even for the rabbit. The rabbit, on the other hand, thought that each hole dug was one hole less that needed digging. When there was no place in the whole field left to dig, the rabbit dug a tunnel to right under where the dog had been lying all that time. There he found the carrot and the bone.

And this is how it was that the dog lost due to his pessimism. Because, thanks to his great instinct, he had already found the right place at the very beginning!

"Optimism is the foundation of courage."

—Nicholas Murray Butler

❑

Perseverance

Meaning

Continued steady belief or efforts, withstanding discouragement or difficulty.

Perseverance helps us keep walking on the same direction without hesitation. It helps us achieve our dreams with a determination that we can achieve what we want.

Story – The Tortoise and the Hare

Once there was a Hare who used to laugh at a Tortoise because he walked along so slowly. "You never can get anywhere with those short legs of yours. Look at my long legs! They're so swift no one would dare race me."

All the animals of field and forest were tired of hearing the Hare brag. At last the Tortoise said, "If we were to run a race, I'm sure I would beat you."

The animals were astonished for they knew the Tortoise was the slowest of them all, and the Hare, bursting into loud laughter, cried, "What a joke! That slowpoke thinks he can beat me! Come on, Mr. Tortoise, you shall see what my feet are made of. Why I can beat you before you are even half-started!"

"You'd better not be too sure," cautioned the Tortoise. All the big and little animals gathered to watch the race. At the signal, the Hare leaped forward in a great bound and soon left the plodding Tortoise far behind him on the dusty road. Looking back, the Hare could not even see the Tortoise after a little while.

"Hum-m, I've as good as won this race already," he thought, "There's really no reason to hurry." So, as the sun was very warm, he decided to rest a bit under a shady tree. "I'll come in away ahead of that Tortoise, anyhow," he told himself. Soon he was sound asleep. The little rest stretched into a good long nap. Meantime, the Tortoise jogged steadily along on the hot, dusty road, ever so slowly, but surely, and soon he passed the Hare who was still peacefully sleeping.

Quietly the Tortoise plodded on nearing the goal. When the Hare finally woke up with a start, he saw the Tortoise just reaching the finish line far ahead and he could hear all the animals cheering the winner.

Boastful and careless, the Hare had lost the race. Now he would never again be able to count on his speed.

Great works are performed not by strength but by perseverance.

—Samuel Johnson

❑

Quality

Meaning

An essential or distinctive characteristic, property, or attribute.

It is important to possess a distinct quality that sets you apart from rest of the group.

Story

The annual school science fair was about to happen a month later, and all the students were busy preparing their models for the competition. The winner would have a chance to visit the national science museum.

Ram was an average student; nobody ever thought that he would create something great some day. Every evening Ram would go into his room and would stay there for hours. His mother started to get worried as to what he was busy doing.

So she went up to his room and saw that Ram was busy building up a model that looked something like a roller coaster, on her enquiring he said that he was creating a model for the science fair.

Although he was an average student and never scored great marks, science was still his favourite subject. When his fellow classmates heard that he too was participating in the science fair, they made fun of him.

So Ram worked harder on his project.

On the day of the fair, Ram displayed his model; the model was a weird looking machine which would show him a particular event of the past or the present when he would feed a particular date or time.

And everybody was amazed to see his model. Ram was a hard working boy, and his quality of hard work set him apart from everybody in that fair, and also led him to win the first prize.

"You have to be first, different or great."

—Loretta Lyn

❑

Responsibility

Meaning

Answerable or accountable, as for something within one's power or control.

It is essential to take responsibility for the actions that we perform, as they can impact anybody and everybody around us.

Story

A young Queen was given a special present from a great wizard. It was a magic chest which would bring happiness to the whole kingdom whenever it was opened in a place where there was a spirit of generosity.

The Queen travelled all over her kingdom, looking for the most generous people. When she had collected them all, she opened the magic chest. However, nothing whatsoever happened.

That was, until one day when, returning to her castle, the Queen saw a poor little boy begging. The Queen would have given the boy some money, but she didn't have any with her. So the boy asked her if she could give him the old chest she had, so he could sell it for a little money, in town. At first the Queen hesitated, because she had been told the chest was magic. But on seeing how poor the boy was, she gave it to him. The boy took the chest and opened it.

Immediately, all the wonderful things one could imagine started flying out of the chest, accompanied by the sound of singing: "Why look for it in others? Goodness always starts in yourself," went the song.

And as well as enjoying all the wonders of the magic chest, the Queen learned to set an example in virtue, and she became the best Queen ever to reign over that kingdom.

Theprice of greatness isresponsibility

"Life is a gift, and it offers us the privilege, opportunity, and responsibility to give something back by becoming more."

— Anthony Robbins

Success

Meaning

The favourable outcome of something attempted.

Success means achieving the goals and objectives that you had set for yourself. It brings confidence in oneself. Success helps us know that we can perform a task well and also teaches us not to be deterred by failures.

Story

A young man asked God the secret of Success. God told the young man to meet him near the river the next morning. They met.

God asked the young man to walk with him towards the river. When the water got up to their neck, God took the young man by surprise and ducked him into the water. The man struggled to get out but God was strong and kept him there until he started turning blue. The young man struggled hard and finally managed to get out and the first thing he did was to gasp and take deep breath.

God asked, "What you wanted the most when you were there?"

The man replied "Air".

God said, "That's the secret to success. When you want success as badly as you wanted air, you will get it. There is no other secret".

"Judge your success by what you had to give up in order to get it".

– Anonymous

❑

Team

Meaning

A group of people organized to work together. A team helps us to perform our work more efficiently and effectively. It is important to work in a team because that helps us achieve more.

Story

A flock of hungry pigeons were flying across the sky in search of food. Having travelled a long distance, they felt tired and settled down on a tree. Just below the tree, they saw grains strewn all over the ground. The pigeons were happy to have found enough food to eat. All the pigeons came down from the tree and started eating the grains. As they were doing so, a huge net fell on them and trapped them all.

The pigeons were taken aback. They noticed a hunter sitting at a distance from the tree, a bow and arrow in hand. The pigeons realized it was the hunter who had attracted them by strewing the grains and it was he who had trapped them in the net. The hunter got up and began to move towards the pigeons.

The leader of the pigeons spoke, "Friends, we are in great trouble. The hunter will catch us if we do not act swiftly in a few seconds. There is only one option available at this moment. Let all of us use our force together and fly up along with the net. If all of us use our force and fly together, we can fly carrying the net along with us. Let us start now."

All the pigeons agreed with him and flew high carrying the net along with them. After travelling sufficient distance away from the hunter, the pigeons settled on a tree and carefully came out of the net one by one and thus escaped the hunter.

"Individually, we are one drop. Together, we are an ocean."

—Ryunosuke Satoro

❑

Unity

Meaning

Something whole or complete that is composed of separate parts.

Story – United We Stand: Divided We Fall

In the middle of the jungle, there stood a big *peepal* tree. A pair of sparrows lived on one of its branches. They had built a strong and comfortable nest and had two beautiful nestlings. They roamed the whole day in the jungle, collecting food to feed their young ones in the evening.

One day a huge elephant came to take rest under that big tree. He was hungry. So he tore off the branch on which the sparrows had built their nest. The branch fell on to the ground and the young ones of the birds were killed.

When the sparrows returned home in the evening, they found their young ones dead. They saw a big elephant lying under the tree and taking rest. Everything became crystal clear now. The elephant was the cause of the death of their loved young ones. The mother sparrow was grief-stricken. She began wailing over the loss of her nestlings.

Seeing her weeping bitterly, a woodpecker, who lived in a nearby tree, came to her to know the reason of her sorrow. The sparrows narrated the whole story. They expressed their wish to take revenge upon the elephant, for his cruel act. They wanted to see him dead.

"You're right", said the woodpecker. "This elephant has no consideration for others. He might, one day, kill my young ones too. Come with me. There is a sweet honey bee around here who's my friend. She is very intelligent. She might be able to tell us how the cruel elephant can be killed."

Having decided upon this, they went to meet the sweet honey bee. They narrated the whole story to her and expressed their wish to revenge themselves on the rogue. The bee consoled them and said, "Don't worry. I've a plan to kill that elephant. Listen, first I'll go to the elephant and sing a song in his ears. The elephant will close his eyes to listen attentively to my melody and when I have hummed him to sleep, the woodpecker would poke his long beak into the elephant's eyes. This will turn him blind. Once he is blinded our job will be easy. I will go and express my sympathies and tell him to pour a few drops of the extract of a particular plant in his eyes to cure them. The elephant will go to fetch that plant. There will be a huge pit full of water lying on his way to the plant. When the elephant goes to collect the plant, he will fall into the pit. Since he will not be able to come out of it, he will die."

Then, as planned, the honey bee sang a song into the ears of the elephant. The elephant closed his eyes to listen to the melody more intently, and the woodpecker, without losing a single moment, made him blind by pecking at his eyes.

The cruel elephant shrieked with pain. He began crying—"Oh, I have lost my eyes. I cannot see anything. Is there anyone who can help me?"

Immediately, thereafter, the honey bee again flew to the elephant, who on the advice of the bee set out to fetch the miraculous plant. But in the way the blind elephant fell into the pit and died.

Thus, the cock and the hen, sparrows avenged the untimely death of their young ones and by causing death to the cruel and foolish elephant, they saved many more lives of innocent creatures.

"Even the weak become strong when they are united."

— Friedrich Schiller

❑

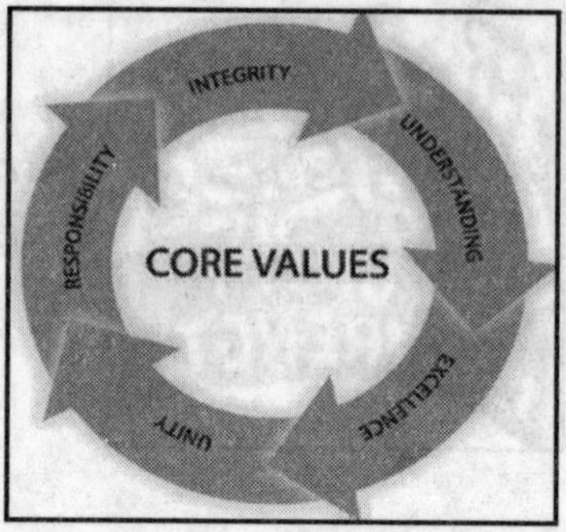

Values

Meaning

Ethical values, the knowledge of what is right and what is wrong.

It is important to have moral values, as they help us do what is right and also lets us differentiate between right and wrong.

Story

Once upon a time, there lived a girl named Meena. Her mother taught her right values since she was a child. When Meena was growing up, she saw that everybody around her would lie or fight with each other.

But her mother had taught her that lying is bad and also you should never fight with anybody. And people would tell her that when you are growing up you have to fight and lie. One day Meena was playing in the playground with her friends and she noticed that her friend Lupa was missing.

Then when Meena and her class returned they noticed that everybody was missing something. Meena asked Lupa, "Where was she in the games period?" Lupa said that she wasn't well so she was in the medical room and didn't know who stole from the bags of her classmates.

Same thing happened the next day. This time Meena decided to hide herself in the class when everybody was gone, so that she can catch the thief. And to her amazement she saw Lupa taking out the stuff from the bags.

Meena caught Lupa red-handed and asked her to confess it to the teacher but Lupa said she can't because everybody will punish her. But Meena's mother had tought her that whenever you are in doubt you should always tell your elders because they always have a solution.

So she went to the teacher and told her about Lupa, then the teacher asked Lupa as to why was she stealing from the bags of her friends. Lupa told her teacher that my father has lost his job and he does not have enough money to buy me pencil and pen.

The teacher thought for a while and then went out of the room. Latter she called Lupa to call her father to school tomorrow as the principal is ready to give her father some work till he doesn't find something himself.

Lupa thanked her teacher and her friend, and never stole from anybody ever again.

Good values, sometimes might not be easy to follow, but remember that they will always help you choose between right and wrong.

Human values should predominate in men's thoughts. Human life has no meaning without these values.

"I am not interested in power for power's sake, but I'm interested in power that is moral, that is right and that is good."

—Martin Luther King, Jr.

❑

Win

Meaning

To finish first in a race, contest, or the like.

To win one has to put in their best efforts. When you work hard nothing can stop you from winning.

Story

Every year, the headmaster of Model School gave a prize to the cleanest classroom in school. "Children, we can win the prize if we work together," said Miss Desai to class 1A. She told the children what they had to do.

"Irfan and Samuel, you take care of the lunch baskets. Arrange them neatly on the shelf at the back of the classroom," she said. Miss Desai asked Sarah, Divya, Arun and Gita to set the desks and benches in order. John and Varsha were told to clean the blackboard. "Please throw rubbish only into the dustbin," said Miss Desai. "And don't forget to dust your desks every day."

The children followed Miss Desai's instructions carefully. She, too, helped the children keep the classroom clean. She put up posters on the walls. The classroom began to look very beautiful and clean. The headmaster came to give a surprise visit to all the classes. And then after a week, he announced the prizes.

"The first prize goes to class 1A!," he said. They have worked hard together to keep their classroom clean.

The students of class 1A jumped with joy. "Hurrah!" they cried.

Miss Desai looked at them proudly. "You worked together to win this prize, children," she said. With hard work you can win anything in life.

Another Story – The Hare and the Lion

A lion was getting fed up of hunting. He called all animals and passed an order, "Everyday one of you should come by yourself as my prey". All animals started to obey this order.

It was the hare's day. The hare was very sad. As he was going to the lion's den, he came across an old well. He looked into it. It was very deep and dangerous. He made a plan to his mind.

The lion was very angry that no animal had come that day. The hare slowly came towards the lion. The lion roared, "Why are you late?" The hare humbly replied, "On my way another lion chased me. I got away with much difficulty to give my life to you, Your Majesty".

The lion was pleased with the hare. But the thought of another lion in the jungle made him angry. The lion roared, "Do you know where he lives?" The hare replied, "Yes Sir. Please come with me".

The hare took the lion to the old well. He said "Sir, that lion lives in this well". The lion peeped into the well. He mistook his reflection for another lion. He roared and there was an echo. He thought that the other lion was roaring too and jumped into the well. That was the end of the lion.

"Your ability to be a winner 100 per cent of the time is based upon giving up the notion that losing at anything is equivalent to being a loser."

– Dr. Wayne W. Dyer

❑

> Excellence is a habit,
> not an act.
> It takes practice and
> perseverance.

X-cellence

Meaning

The state or quality of excelling or being exceptionally good, extreme merit and superiority.

We should always look for excelling at whatever we do.

Story — The Parable of a Pencil

The pencil maker took the pencil aside, just before putting him into the box.

"There are five things you need to know," he told the pencil, "Before I send you out into the world. Always remember them and never forget, and you will become the best pencil you can be."

One: "You will be able to do many great things, but only if you allow yourself to be held in someone's hand."

Two: "You will experience a painful sharpening from time to time, but you'll need it to become a better pencil."

Three: "You will be able to correct any mistakes you might make."

Four: "The most important part of you will always be what's inside."

And Five: "On every surface you are used on, you must leave your mark. No matter what the condition, you must continue to write."

The pencil understood and promised to remember, and went into the box with purpose in its heart.

Now replacing the place of the pencil with you. Always remember them and never forget, and you will become the best person you can be.

One: "You will be able to do many great things, but only if you allow yourself to be held in God's hand. And allow other human beings to access you for the many gifts you possess."

Three: "You will be able to correct any mistakes you might make."

Allow this parable on the pencil to encourage you to know that you are a special person and only you can fulfil the purpose to which you were born to accomplish.

"We are what we repeatedly do. Excellence, then, is not an act, but a habit."

—Aristotle

❑

Youth

Meaning

The appearance, freshness, vigour, spirit, etc. – characteristic of one who is young.

The young has a power of moving the course of action according to their will. The vigour could be used to turn the world into a better place.

Story – Bhagat Singh

The young Bhagat Singh was brought up in a politically charged state of Punjab. The occurrence of the *Jallianwala* massacre in 1919 killed more than 400 innocent lives and thousands of people were injured. Bhagat Singh went to the park of Jallianwala to collect soil from the park and kept it for life.

In 1928, the British Government appointed a commission under the leadership of Sir John Simon to report the political events.

In Lahore, India, Lala Lajpatrai and Pundit Mohan protested again the commission. This was a silent protest and Chief Scott had banned the meeting, Scott beat Lala Lajpatrai many times with a *lathi*, which was a bamboo stick. Bhagat Singh had witnessed this scene and he took revenge with the help of Chandra Shekar, Rajguru and Sukhdev whose aim was to kill Scott.

Mr. Sanders, a junior officer, was killed instead due to a mistake in their identity. Bhagat Singh had to escape from Lahore to get away from death punishment.

On April 8, 1929 at Delhi Central Assembly, Bhagat Singh had volunteered to throw a bomb in the middle of the Assembly where a meeting to pass a law was being held.

The bomb was planned carefully not to cause death or injury but to grab the government's attention that the form of control was not going to be tolerated no more.

Bhagat Singh and Batukeshwar Dutt were arrested after throwing the bomb.

Bhagat Singh thought the court would be a proper place to get publicity for the cause of freedom, and did not want to deny the crime.

But he gave a fiery statement giving reasons for killing which was representation of freedom struggle. He wanted to be shot like a soldier, and not die at the gallows.

But his plea was rejected, and he was hung on 23rd of March 1931.

"Youth has no age."

—Pablo Picasso

❑

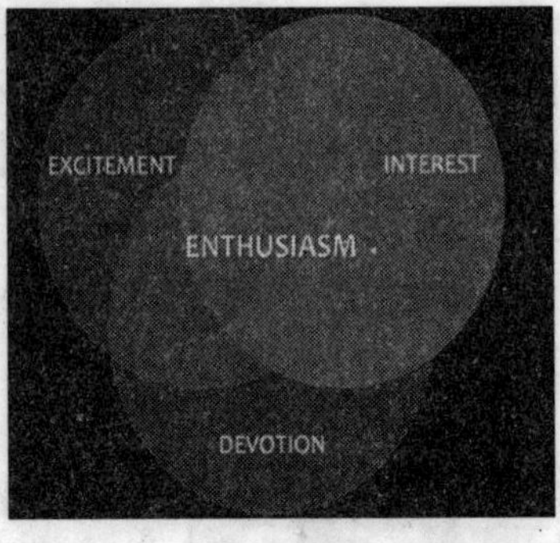

Zeal

Meaning

Eager desire or endeavour; enthusiastic diligence.

One should always work with zeal. When your work is full of zeal and enthusiasm, you always achieve great results.

Story

One hot day, a thirsty crow flew all over the fields looking for water. For a long time, she could not find any. She felt very weak, almost giving up hope.

Suddenly, she saw a water jug below her. She flew straight down to see if there was any water inside. Yes, she could see some water inside the jug!

The crow tried to push her head into the jug. Sadly, she found that the neck of the jug was too narrow. Then she tried to push the jug down for the water to flow out. She found that the jug was too heavy.

The crow thought hard for a while. Then looking around her, she saw some pebbles. She suddenly had a good idea. She started picking up the pebbles one by one, dropping each into the jug. As more and more pebbles filled the jug, the water level kept rising. Soon it was high enough for the crow to drink. Her plan had worked!

If you try hard enough, you may soon find an answer to your problem.

Through zeal, knowledge is gotten; through lack of zeal, knowledge is lost; let a man who knows the double path of gain and loss thus place himself that knowledge may grow.

—Buddha

❑

PART - II

Inspirational Stories

Love and Compassion

In order to renovate the house, someone in Japan tore open the wall. Japanese houses normally have a hollow space between the wooden walls. When tearing down the walls, he found that there was a lizard stuck there because a nail from outside was hammered into one of its feet. He saw this, felt pity, and at the same time he was curious. When he checked the nail, turns out, it was nailed 10 years ago when the house was first built.

What happened?

The lizard had survived in such a position for 10 years! In a dark wall partition for 10 years without moving, it is impossible and mind boggling. Then he wondered how this lizard survived for 10 years without moving a single step—since its foot was nailed!

So he stopped his work and observed the lizard, what it had been doing, and what and how it has been eating. Later, not knowing from where it came, appeared another lizard, with food in its mouth.

Ahh!

He was stunned and rat the same time, touched deeply. Another lizard had been feeding the stuck one for the past 10 years....

Such love, such a beautiful love! Such love happened with this tiny creature.... What can love do?

It can do wonders! Love can do miracles! Just think about it; one lizard had been feeding the other one untiringly for 10 long years, without giving up hope on its partner. If a small creature like a lizard can love like this.... just imagine how we can love if we try.

"Be kind whenever possible. It is always possible."

—Dalai Lama

❑

Definiteness of Purpose

Bob Christopher has definiteness of purpose with Positive Mental Power.

He wanted to go around the world in 80 days. He said, "I used to daydream a great deal but when I grew older, I read two books on motivation: Think and grow rich and the magic of believing".

Around the world in 80 days, now why couldn't! go around the world on $ 80 believed that any given aim could be accomplished if had faith and confidence that it could be. That is: If I started from where was to get go to where I wanted to be. Thought: Others had worked on freighters to earn their transatlantic passages and hitchhiked all over the world, so why couldn't I.

And he took a pen from his pocket and wrote on a piece of a note paper a list of the problems with which he could have faced. Also, he made notes of what he thought were workable answers to each.

Now Bob is a professional photographer and he did have a camera. And he went into action and

- Entered into contact with Pfizer Company, to collect soil samples from the various countries he intended to visit....
- Obtained an international driver's license and a set of maps in return for a promised report on Middle East road conditions.
- Arranged for youth hostel membership.
- Contacted a freight airline which agreed to transport him by plane over the Atlantic on his promise to obtain.
- Photographs which the company intended to use for publicity.

When his plans were completed, this young boy of 26 left New York City by plane with $80.00 in his pocket. Around the world in $80.00 was his definite major aim. He had following experiences:

- Had breakfast at Newfoundland. He photographed at the cooks and they were pleased who in turn gave him breakfast.
- Bought four cartoons of American Cigarettes at Ireland that cost him $4.80.

At that time cigarettes were as good as money—a medium of exchange in many of the countries.

- Arrived at Vienna from Paris. The fee—one cartoon of cigarette to the driver.
- Rode a bus to Damascus. A policeman in Syria was so proud of the picture that Bob has taken of him he ordered bus driver to take him.
- Took the photograph of president and staff of Iraq Express Transportation Company. This earned ride from Baghdad to Tehran.
- In Bangkok, the owner of a very fine restaurant fed him like a king. Bob gave him the information he wanted detailed description of a specific area and set of maps.
- He was brought from Japan to San Francisco as a crew member of S.S.—The Flying Spray.

So, he went around the world in $80.00 in 84 days—because he had definiteness of purpose with Positive Mental Attitude.

We can also achieve anything—if there is definiteness of purpose with positive mental attitude.

Hope is magic ingredient in motivating yourself and others.

The story goes that some time ago, a man punished his 5-year-old daughter for wasting a roll of expensive gold wrapping paper. Money was tight, and he became even more upset when the child pasted the gold paper so as to decorate a box to put under the Christmas tree.

Nevertheless, the little girl brought the gift box to her father the next morning and said, "This is for you, Daddy." The father was embarrassed by his earlier overreaction, but his anger flared again when he found the box was empty. He spoke to her in a harsh manner, "Don't you know, young lady, when you give someone a present there's supposed to be something inside the package?"

The little girl looked up at him with tears in her eyes and said, "Daddy, it's not empty. I blew kisses into it until it was full." The father was crushed.... He fell on his knees and put his arms around his little girl, and he begged her to forgive him for his unnecessary anger....

An accident took the life of the child only a short time later, and it is told that the father kept that gold box by his bed for all the years of his life. And whenever he was discouraged or faced difficult problems, he open the box and take out an imaginary kiss and remember the love of the child who had put it there.

In a very real sense, each of us as human beings have been given a golden box filled with unconditional love and kisses from our children, family and friends. There is no other more precious possession anyone could hold.

❑

Follow Your Dreams

There were once two brothers who lived on the 80th level. On coming home one day, they realized to their dismay that the lifts were not working and that they had to climb the stairs home. After struggling to the 20th level, fainting and tired, they decided to abandon their bags. They left their bags there and climbed on. When they struggled to the 40th level, the younger brother started to grumble and both of them began to quarrel. They continued to climb the flights of steps, quarrelling all the way to the 60th floor.

They then realized that they had only 20 levels more to climb and decided to stop quarrelling and continue climbing in peace.

They silently climbed on and reached their home at last. Each stood calmly before the door and waited for the other to open the door. And they realized that the key was in their bags which were left on the 20th floor.

This story is a reflection on our lives. Many of us, during childhood days, live as per the expectations of our parents, teachers and friends. We seldom get to do the things that we really like or love. It is under so much pressure and stress, that by our early 20s we get tired and decide to dump this load and enjoy life. Being free of the stress and pressure, we start working enthusiastically.

But by the time we reach our 40s, we start to lose our vision and along with that our dreams and goal in life. We begin to feel dissatisfied and start to complain and criticize. On reaching 60, we realize that we have little time left for complaining and we begin to walk the final path in peace and calmness. We think that there is nothing left that could disappoint us, only to realize that we cannot rest in peace because we have an unfulfilled dream. A dream we abandoned about 60 plus years ago.

So what is your dream? Keep them alive. Follow your dreams so that you do not live with regrets and you will have wonderful stories to share with your loved ones.

"No matter how dark things seem to be or actually are, raise your sights and see the possibilities—always see them, for they're always there."

—Norman Vincent Peale

❑

How You React

10% of life is made up of what happens to you.

90% of life is decided by how you react.

What does this mean?

We really have no control over 10% of what happens to us. We cannot stop the car from breaking down. The plane may be arriving late, which throws our whole schedule off. A driver may cut us off in traffic. We have no control over this 10%. The other 90% is different. You determine the other 90%. How? By your reaction!

You cannot control a red light, but you can control your reaction. Let us look at an everyday example.

You're eating breakfast with your family. Your

daughter knocks over a cup of coffee onto your business shirt. You have no control over what just happened.

What happens next will be determined by how you react. You curse. You harshly scold your daughter for knocking the coffee cup over. She breaks down in tears. After scolding her, you turn to your spouse and criticize them for placing the cup too close to the edge of the table. A short verbal battle follows. You storm upstairs and change your shirt. Back downstairs you find your daughter has been too busy crying to finish breakfast and get ready for school. She misses the bus. Your spouse must leave immediately for work. You rush to the car and drive your daughter to school. Because you are late, you drive 40 miles an hour in a 30 mph speed limit. After a 15 minute delay and throwing ₹ 100 as a penalty to a traffic policeman for overspeeding, you reach office. In the evening, you look forward to going back home. When you arrive home, you find small wedge in your relationship with your spouse and daughter.

Why? Because of how you reacted in the morning.

Why did you have a bad day?

(a) Did the coffee cause it?
(b) Did your daughter cause it?
(c) Did the policeman cause it?
(d) Did you cause it?

The answer is (d).

You had no control over what happened with the coffee. How you reacted in those five seconds is what caused your bad day.

Here is what could have and should have happened. Coffee splashes over you. Your daughter is about to cry. You gently say, "It's OK honey, you just need to be more careful next time". Grabbing a towel you rush upstairs. After grabbing a new shirt and your briefcase. You come back down in time, look through the window and see your child getting on the bus. She turns and waves. You and your spouse embrace each other before you both go to work. You arrive five minutes early and cheerfully greet the staff. Your boss comments on how good of day, you are having.

Notice the Difference

Two different scenarios. Both started the same way. Both ended differently. Why? Because of how you REACTED. You really do not have any control over 10% of what happens. The other 90% is determined by your reaction. Here are some ways to apply the 90/10 secret. If someone says something negative about you, do not be a sponge. Let the attack roll off like water on glass. You don't have to let the negative comment affect you! React properly or it will not ruin your day. A wrong reaction could result in losing a friend, being fired, getting stressed out, etc. How do you react if someone cuts you off in traffic? Do you lose your temper? Pound the steering wheel? Do you curse? Does your blood pressure skyrocket? Do you try and bump them?

Who cares if you arrive ten seconds later at work? Why let the blue car ruin your drive? Why lose sleep or get irritated? It will work out.

The plane is late. It is going to mangle your schedule for the day. Why take out your frustration on the flight attendant? He has no control over what is going on. Use your time to study, get to know the other passenger, etc. Why get stressed out? It will just make things worse.

"Our best friends and our worst enemies are our thoughts. A thought can do us more good than a doctor or banker or a faithful friend. It can also do us more harm than a brick".

– Dr. Frank Crane

❑

Win through Actions not through Arguments

In 1688, Wren designed a magnificent town hall for the city of Westminster. The Mayor, however, was not satisfied; in fact, he was nervous. He told Wren he was afraid that the second floor was not secure and that it could all come crashing down on his office on the first floor. He demanded that Wren add two extra stone columns for extra support. Wren, the consummate Engineer, knew that these columns could serve no purpose and that the Mayor fears were baseless. But he built them and the Mayor was grateful.

It was only years later that workmen on a high scaffold saw that the columns stopped short of ceiling.

They were dummies. But both men got what they wanted. The Mayor could relax, and Wren knew posterity would understand that original design worked and the columns were unnecessary.

The moral of the story – Win through Actions not through Arguments.

"In the middle of difficulty lies opportunity."

– Albert Einstein

❑

We are Poor – Not Because of God

S. B. Fuller was one of the seven children of a Negro tenant farmer. He started to work at the age of five. By the time he was nine, he was driving mules. There was nothing unusual on this; the children of most of the tenant farmers went to work early. These families accepted poverty as their lot and asked for no better.

Young Fuller was different from his friends in one way; he had a remarkable mother. His mother refused to accept this hand-to-mouth existence for her children, though it was all she had ever known. She knew there was something wrong with the fact that her family was barely getting along in a world of joy and plenty. She used to talk to her son about her dreams.

"We should not be poor, S.B.," she used to say. And don't let me hear you say that it is God's Will that we are poor. We are poor—not because of God. We are poor because father has never developed a desire to become rich. No one in our family has ever developed a desire to be anything else.

With this message in mind. S.B. Fuller became one of the most successful men in USA. He said, "You have everything to gain and I have nothing to lose by trying. Success is achieved and maintained by those who keep trying."

"If you think you can, you can. If you think you can't, you can't. Either way you are right!"

—Mary Kay Ash

❑

Learn through Chanakya's Teachings

Chanakya taught people to learn good things from animals – lion, cock, dog and donkey.

What are they?

Lion

1. Whether it is big or small, one must do very work with full capacity and power. He never does anything half-heartedly.

Cock

1. Cock gets up at right time.
2. Fights bitterly.

3. Makes its enemy to flee.
4. Usurpation devours their share also.

Dog

1. A dog drives satisfaction out of a little eating.
2. Sleeps very alert.
3. Alert despite up being in great slumber.
4. Faithfulness.
5 Bravery.
6. Always alert save his master.

Donkey

1. Capacity to carry the load.
2. To work in spite of being bone tired.
3. Getting satisfaction in all conditions.

"I kept six honest serving men. They taught me all I knew. Their names are What and Why and When and How and Where and Who."

—Rudyard Kipling

❑

Japanese Fish

The Japanese have always loved fresh fish. But the waters close to Japan have not held many fish for decades. So to feed the Japanese population, fishing boats got bigger and went farther than ever. The farther the fishermen went, the longer it took to bring in the fish. If the return trip took more than a few days, the fish were not fresh. The Japanese did not like the taste. To solve this problem, fishing companies installed freezers on their boats. They would catch the fish and freeze them at sea. Freezers allowed the boats to go farther and stay longer. However, the Japanese could taste the difference between fresh and frozen and they did not like frozen fish.

The frozen fish brought a lower price. So fishing companies installed fish tanks. They would catch the fish and stuff them in the tanks, fin to fin. After a little thrashing around, the fish topped moving. They were tired and dull, but alive. Unfortunately, the Japanese could still taste the difference. Because the fish did not move for days, they lost their fresh fish taste. The Japanese preferred the lively taste of fresh fish, not sluggish fish.

So how did Japanese fishing companies solve this problem? How do they get fresh-tasting fish to Japan? If you were consulting the fish industry, what would you recommend? As soon as you reach your goals such as finding a wonderful mate, starting a successful company, paying off your debts or whatever, you might lose your passion. You don't need to work so hard so you relax. You experience the same problem as lottery winners who waste their money, wealthy heirs who never grow up and bored homemakers who get addicted to prescription drugs. Like the Japanese fish problem, the best solution is simple. It was observed by L. Ron Hubbard in the early 1950s. "Man thrives, oddly enough, only in the presence of a challenging environment." The Benefits of a Challenge: The more intelligent, persistent and competent you are, the more you enjoy a good problem. If your challenges are the correct size, and if you are steadily conquering those challenges, you are happy. You think of your challenges and get energized. You are excited to try new solutions. You have fun. You are alive! How Japanese Fish Stay Fresh: To keep the fish tasting fresh, the Japanese fishing companies still put the fish in the tanks. But now they add a small shark to each tank. The shark eats a few fish, but most of the fish arrive in a very lively state. The fish are challenged.

Instead of avoiding challenges, jump into them. Beat the heck out of them. Enjoy the game. If your challenges are too large or too numerous, do not give up. Failing makes you tired. Instead, reorganize. Find more determination, more knowledge, more help. If you have met your goals, set some bigger goals. Once you meet your personal or family needs, move onto goals for your group, the society, even mankind. Don't create success and lie in it. You have resources, skills and abilities to make a difference. So, put a shark in your tank and see how far you can really go!

"I've missed more than 9000 shots in my career. I've lost almost 300 games. 26 times, I've been trusted to take the game winning shot and missed. I've failed over and over and over again in my life. And that is why, I succeed."

—Michael Jordan

❑

Luck is not Always by Chance

Why do some people get all the luck while others never get the Breaks they deserve? A psychologist, Professor Richard Wiseman from University of Hertfordshire says he has discovered the answer.

Ten years ago, I set out to examine luck. I wanted to know why some people are always in the right place at the right time, while others consistently experience ill-fortune. I placed advertisements in national newspapers asking for people who felt consistently lucky or unlucky to contact me.

Hundreds of extraordinary men and women volunteered for my research and, over the years,

I have interviewed them, monitored their lives and had them take part in experiments. The results reveal that although these people have almost no insight into the causes of their luck, their thoughts and behaviour are responsible for much of their good and bad fortune. Take the case of seemingly chance opportunities. Lucky people consistently encounter such opportunities, whereas unlucky people do not.

I carried out a simple experiment to discover whether this was due to differences in their ability to spot such opportunities. I gave both lucky and unlucky people a newspaper, and asked them to look through it and tell me how many photographs were inside. I had secretly placed a large message halfway through the newspaper saying: "Tell the experimenter you have seen this and win 250 pounds."

This message took up half of the page and was written in type that was more than two inches high. It was staring everyone straight in the face, but the unlucky people tended to miss it and the lucky people tended to spot it. Unlucky people are generally tenser than lucky people, and this anxiety disrupts their ability to notice the unexpected.

As a result, they miss opportunities because they are too focused on looking for something else. They go to parties intending on finding their perfect partner and so miss opportunities to make good friends. They look through newspapers determined to find certain types of job advertisements and miss other types of jobs. Lucky people are more relaxed and open, and therefore see what is there rather than just what they are looking for. My research eventually revealed that lucky people generate good fortune through four principles. They are skilled at creating and noticing chance opportunities, make lucky decisions by listening to their intuition, create self-fulfilling prophesies via positive expectations and adopt a resilient attitude that transforms bad luck into good.

Towards the end of the work, I wondered whether these principles could be used to create good luck. I asked a group of volunteers to spend a month carrying out exercises designed to help them think and behave like a lucky person.

Dramatic results these exercises helped them spot chance opportunities, listen to their intuition, expect to be lucky, and be more resilient to bad luck. One month later, the volunteers returned and described what had happened. The results were dramatic: 80% of people were now happier, more satisfied with their lives and, perhaps most important of all, luckier.

The lucky people had become even luckier and the unlucky had become lucky. Finally, I had found the elusive "Luck Factor". Here are Professor

Wiseman's four top tips for becoming lucky:

1. Listen to your gut instincts—they are normally right.
2. Be open to new experiences and breaking your normal routine.
3. Spend a few moments each day remembering things that went well.
4. Visualize yourself being lucky before an important meeting or telephone call. Luck is very often a self-fulfilling prophecy.

"Have a Lucky Day!!"

❑

Be A Winner

A winner is not one who never fails, but one who NEVER QUITS!

A candidate for a news broadcasters post was rejected by officials since his voice was not fit for a news broadcaster. He was also told that with his obnoxiously long name, he would never be famous. He is **Amitabh Bachchan**.

A small boy – the fifth amongst seven siblings of a poor father, was selling newspapers in a small village to earn his living. He was not exceptionally smart at school but was fascinated by religion and rockets. The first rocket he built crashed. A missile that he built crashed multiple times and he was ridiculed. He is the person to have scripted the Space

Odyssey of India single-handedly, i.e. **Dr. A.P.J. Abdul Kalam**.

In 1962, four nervous young musicians played their first record audition for the executives of the Decca Recording Company.

The executives were not impressed. While turning down this group of musicians, one executive said, "We don't like their sound. Groups of guitars are on the way out."

The group was called **The Beatles**.

In 1944, Emmeline Snively, Director of the Blue Book Modelling Agency told modelling hopeful Norma Jean Baker, "You'd better learn secretarial work or else get married." She went on and became **Marilyn Monroe.**

In 1954, Jimmy Denny, Manager of the Grand Ole Opry, fired a singer after one performance. He told him, "You aren't going nowhere son. You ought to go back to driven' a truck." He went on to become **Elvis Presley**.

When **Thomas Edison** invented the light bulb, he tried over 2000 experiments before he got it to work. A young reporter asked him how it felt to fail so many times. He said, "I never failed once. I invented the light bulb. It just happened to be a 2000-step process."

In the 1940s, another young inventor named **Chester Carlson** took his idea to 20 operations, including some of the biggest in the country. They all turned him down. In 1947, after seven long years of rejections, he finally got a tiny company named Haloid to purchase the rights to his invention for an electrostatic paper-copying process. Haloid became Xerox Corporation.

A little girl – the 20th of 22 children, was born prematurely and her survival was doubtful. When she was 4 years old, she contracted double pneumonia and scarlet fever, which left her with a paralysed left leg.

At age 9, she removed the metal leg brace she had been dependent on and began to walk without it. By 13 she had developed a rhythmic walk, which doctors said was a miracle. That same year she decided to become a runner. She entered a race and came in last. For the next few years every race she entered, she came in last. Everyone told her to quit, but she kept on running. One day she actually won a race. And then another. From then on she won every race she entered. Eventually, this little girl, **Wilma Rudolph**, went on to win three Olympic gold medals.

A school teacher scolded a boy for not paying attention to his mathematics and for not being able to solve simple problems. She told him that you would not become anybody in life. The boy went on to become **Albert Einstein**.

"No one can defeat us unless we first defeat ourselves."

—Dwight Eisenhower

❑

Conclusion

If Ever You Need Me

If ever you need me, I'll be right here,
To chase away the sadness, and wipe
away a tear.
If ever you need me, I'll be two steps behind,
To follow in your footsteps, and hear what's on
your mind.
If ever you need me, you'll never have to fear,
That your presence isn't important, and your
love isn't dear.
If ever you need me, I'll always be around,
To bring back the laughter, where deep in your
heart it's found.
You'll never have to worry, for I'll
always be here.

I AM HERE FOR YOU!

❑

Words Have Power: Self-Talk for Success

The most powerful words of all are the ones you say to yourself every day. Specifically, I mean the self-talk or conversation that you have with yourself throughout the day. Have you ever stopped to listen to how you talk to yourself? I have noticed that people say things to themselves that they would never say to someone else.

Words have power and they have a tremendous impact on your health. Do you ever hear yourself say, "I don't have time to exercise," or "Just one more won't hurt"?, Do you frequently say "I'm tired" or "I'm stressed"? Words like these create the emotion or feeling that you would have if the words were true. These emotions lead to the actions reflected by your feelings, which then reinforce the feelings.

If you say you are tired, then you will begin to feel tired. Feeling tired leads to sluggish behaviour which generates fatigue rather than vibrant energy. What you focus on grows. If you focus on feeling unhealthy then you will tend to have unhealthy behaviours that follow.

❑

Words Have Power: Program Your Health with the Right Words

The words you use are like computer code that becomes the software of your mind. You program your behaviour with your words. **If you don't like the results that you are getting in your life, you simply need to change the software by reprogramming your mind.** It takes time to work out the bugs in a program, but the goal is consciously to decide what you want, use words and thoughts consistent with that desire, and then began acting on the thought.

For example, if you want to be thin, you first need to change the words you use. Stop saying and stop thinking, "I'm fat." Replace that thought with

"I enjoy being a healthy weight" or "I am enjoying the process of becoming thin." Expand on this by changing the conversations in your head about food and exercise.

❑

Words Have Power: Talk Healthy—Think Healthy

Cultivate positive self-talk that leads to healthier thinking. Think, "Healthy people eat vegetables instead of cake," and "Thin people exercise most days of the week, so I will go to the gym today". Squash all thoughts that are contrary to your goal and cultivate those that lead to healthy behaviours. Start thinking of yourself as a healthy person, start speaking healthy words and then take healthy actions.

❑

Words Have Power: Your Words are an Indication of Your Thoughts

Your words indicate your thoughts. **A word is a thought revealed.** What you say determines your destiny as much as what you think.

Positive thinking and positive speech are like the chicken and egg analogy. On the one hand, positive thinking leads to positive speech. On the other hand, positive speech leads to positive thinking.

The important thing to remember is that the power of positive speech and the power of positive thinking go together. Positive thinking is nullified by negative talk. Positive talk is nullified by negative thought. Having one without the other is like attempting to fly with a broken wing. The two must be in harmony.

❑

Words Have Power: Your Words Create Your Destiny

Realize that your words reinforce your thinking. The converse is true—your thoughts reinforce your words. **The power of positive thinking is reinforced by positive speech.**

Your words have power in them. I know there are some that don't agree with this, but there are spiritual laws at work that affect you whether you recognize them or not. What you believe does not change the truth. The law of gravity works whether you believe in it or not. The law of getting what you speak works—whether you believe in it or not.

Even if you don't believe it, why take chances? Take the safe route. Say the right things. If you can change your thinking and talking to be in line with your dreams, then you are on your way to achieving them.

"Words call forth emotions and are universally the means by which we influence. Words can give the greatest happiness or bring utter despair!," says Sigmund Freud

The key then, is to speak only those things that you desire for yourself. Whatever is not in harmony with your dreams, do not say it. Learn to use the power of positive thinking and positive speech. This takes practice and patience.

Practice every day. Before long, it will become a part of you. You will be more amazed at the difference it will make in YOUR life. Success, riches, health and a fulfilling life will be within your reach. You will see the results. Persist. Never give up. The power of positive thinking will help you through.

YOU CAN DO IT ALL. YOU CAN DO IT: 24×7
THINK POSITIVE, THINK POSSIBLE!
THINK OPTIONS, THINK SOLUTIONS!!

Words Have Power....

❑❑❑